Creating Designs
With
Dried Flowers

by Harold C. Cook

An *ideals* Publication
First Printing

ISBN 0-89542-288-3 295

Ideals Publishing Corporation
Milwaukee, Wisconsin 53226

Editorial Director, James Kuse
Managing Editor, Ralph Luedtke
Photographic Editor, Gerald Koser
Production Editor, Stuart Zyduck
Consulting Editor, Lorraine Obst

Contents

Preface   5

Methods of Drying   6
    Drying in a Desiccant   9
    Steps in Drying with Silica Gel   10
    Drying Plant Materials in Sand   14
    Drying the Microwave Way   15
    Comments on Other Desiccants   17
    Air Drying   18

Preserving Plant Materials in Glycerine   21

The Mechanics of Flower Arranging   27
    Dried Arrangements in Glass Domes   35
    Wall Hangings and Plaques   37
    Designs with an Oriental Influence   38

Pressing Plant Materials   40
    Pressed Flower Portraits   42

The Not-So-Lowly Marigold   43

Roadside and Native Materials   45
    Gourds: Growing and Curing   47
    All About Corn   50
    Preserving and Tinting Corn Husks   53
    Corn Husk Flowers   54
    Hedge Apple Flowers   61

In Conclusion . . .   64

A rhythmic pattern is created by using the barren branches of the Japanese Fantail Willow arranged in a handcrafted shell design lead bowl. Silica gel was used to dry the early spring jonquils. After drying, the jonquils were sprayed with several coats of DMP to act as a moisture barrier.

Preface

Planting, growing and arranging flowers is practically the story of my life from the time I was a first grader in Galesburg, Illinois. My earliest recollection was potting a violet from the garden of my first grade teacher as a gift to my mother on Mother's Day 1918. Then we moved to Princeton. During my high school years, I worked in a greenhouse, reading all the gardening and flower arranging books in the school and local library in order to learn more about floriculture and horticulture. After I graduated from high school, we moved to Dixon. These were depression years, but I somehow managed to keep busy mowing lawns and weeding gardens. In 1932 I established a small nursery, and in 1939 opened my flower shop.

For years I gathered dried roadside plant materials for autumn and winter arrangements and combined contorted branches with fresh flowers to create interesting designs. With the advent of silica gel as a drying desiccant for flowers, I became interested in experimenting in flower drying. A few years ago when I was advised to curtail my strenuous activities in the floral business, I turned my attention to the potentials in the field of flower drying. It wasn't long before I found it so fascinating that I was urged to add this subject to my list of lectures. Now my classes and workshops on flower drying are filled to capacity, months in advance. It is a rewarding experience to see how interested the members of my classes become in collecting, drying and arranging plant materials—and how interested they are in growing varieties of plants that are compatible for their personal use. I have found that good gardeners usually make good neighbors; and good neighbors make a better and healthier community in which to live.

If I were to dedicate this book it would be to the memory of my dear mother. She was so kind and considerate in overlooking the inconvenience of having every conceivable space on tables, chairs and corners piled high with boxes of drying flowers. Even our dining room chandelier and our closets were loaded with air-drying flowers on hangers. I know she always breathed a sigh of relief when the drying season was over, and the flowers were stored away for later use. Then she would often invite her friends to come in during the drab winter months to share the beauty these dried flowers brought to our home.

Methods
of Drying

Flower drying is by no means a new fad or craze. The colonists brought this art from their native lands and began practicing it while our country was in its infancy. Historians tell us that the Egyptians, Greeks and Romans used dried plant materials to decorate their temples, villas and homes. Later this art spread through Europe, the British Isles and Scandinavian countries, with nearly all the castles of the wealthy and the cottages of the peasants displaying some form of dried materials in their decorations. For centuries the Japanese have used dried branches, roots, stones, driftwood and other dried plant materials to accent the fresh flower arrangements in their temples and on the altar in their *tokonoma*, a recessed alcove in their living room used for meditation and worship.

In eighteenth-century America, few fresh flowers were used for home decoration except during the outdoor growing season. Flowers from the garden were dried during their blooming season and stored away to be used for decorating during the winter months.

The methods of drying and preserving flowers and other plant materials have changed very little from those used centuries ago. Today, however, new absorption materials are available to hasten the drying process.

Anyone interested in flowers can participate in this fascinating hobby as it does not require any great investment in equipment or supplies and very little, if any, scientific skill. I have found that one learns more by trial and error, plus a great deal of perseverance.

Reserve and dry some of your fresh garden flowers during the growing season to use during the winter season. Flowers dried in a desiccant generally will not hold too well during our warm humid Midwest springs and summers, but seem to hold indefinitely during the winter when the homes are heated and less humid.

You may not have instant success with your first attempts, but failure is always a challenge. It is great therapy and you will soon be richly rewarded with the beauty you have preserved.

During the past few years there has been a great deal of interest in dried materials. Importers have been searching the world over to bring new and exciting dried materials to our markets. Nearly every florist, craft shop and department store has a large selection of both domestic and imported dried plant materials. Many of these purchased materials may be combined with collected native materials to add interest and color to an artistic dried arrangement.

The imported and domestic processed materials are generally hardened by nature so they will not wilt during humid, muggy weather. Most of these materials are gathered after they have been dried and their natural colors usually range from beige to brown. The processors bleach and then tint the material, providing a wide range of decorator colors for the arranger. Even the bleached white materials are very much in demand as a focal point in contemporary interiors.

I urge you to gather and dry as many materials as you can, purchasing only those that are essential to the design—it's a lot more fun, less expensive and gives such personal gratification.

Above: Necessary supplies needed in preserving and drying plant materials and in creating designs.

Supplies

As in all crafts and hobbies, there are a few supplies and materials needed to create the finished designs:

Silica gel for drying

Glycerine for preserving

Bar-fast, Filfast and Styrofoam to support the stems

Cling (floral clay or adhesive)

Sobo, Velverette, Quik for adhesives

Florists green annealed cut wire

Masking or Davey Tape

Florist greening pins

Florist wired wood picks, 2½", 3", 4", 6"

Soft camel's hair brushes

Floratape, ½" and 1" widths, light green, green, twig green, brown

Pruners, wire cutters, tweezers, scissors, knife

Spool or paddle wire

"Floraset Clear," "DMP," or "Cherish," aerosol preservative sprays.

Drying in a Desiccant

Until recently, only two or three materials were used as desiccants in drying plant material. A desiccant is defined as "a substance used to draw out moisture." The earliest recorded desiccant used in flower drying was sand, and this drying medium is still widely used. Another drying medium is a combination of borax and cornmeal, used extensively by our colonists because of the favorable results they had in drying flowers in their native homelands. Combinations of borax and fine sand were also used. Some hobbyists have used borax alone; however, this seems to me to be rather risky and expensive.

Silica Gel

Silica gel is an industrial desiccant that is now widely used to dry and retain the beauty of your choicest blooms. Silica gel is a mixture of fine, white sugar-like crystals sprinkled with tiny cobalt blue indicator crystals. When properly used these amazing crystals will preserve the shape and brilliant colors of your plant material in just a matter of a few days. Silica gel is available at most craft shops, garden centers or shops selling flower arranging supplies. For the beginner, there are kits available containing the basic supplies needed to dry flowers; however, the silica gel in these kits is barely enough to dry more than three or four small to medium-size flowers at one time. For the beginner these kits are fine. However, I suggest a source be located where the silica gel can be purchased in bulk at a savings. As you become more adept in drying flowers, you will find that ten pounds, twenty pounds or even more will not be too much to keep on hand for use during the drying seasons.

Silica gel may seem expensive when you begin your project; but it may be used over and over. The only loss is in the crystals you might lose when sprinkling or pouring off the silica gel or the crystals you have neglected to remove from the dried plant material. The tiny blue indicator crystals will turn pink or white when the moisture capacity of the silica gel has been reached, indicating it is no longer able to draw any additional moisture until reactivated. To reactivate, pour the crystals into a shallow pan and dry in a 250° oven until the indicator crystals return to the original cobalt blue color. Place in an airtight container and allow to cool before using. Always store silica gel in an airtight container in a dry location.

Plant material to be dried should be selected at the peak of perfection. Any blemishes on petals or leaves will be magnified during the drying process. Plant material from the garden should be cut after the sun has thoroughly dried any dew or other moisture that might have settled on it. Select flowers at their peak of bloom, color and development. After several tries you will be able to judge the color the flower will retain during and after the drying process. Purples, dark blues and reds are the most difficult flower colors to dry, as most of these colors lose their brilliance and luminosity. The flower stems must be kept in water from the time they are cut until they are placed in the silica gel. If they are wilted by the time you arrive at the work area, give the stems a fresh cut and immediately place in a container of lukewarm water. Do not use them for drying until they have regained their turgidity. Do not try to dry wilted blooms in silica gel. They must be crisp, firm and heavy with water content.

Any sealable airtight container large enough to adequately contain the flowers will be satisfactory to use in this drying process. I save all types of sealable containers to use for drying: coffee cans, plastic storage containers, cake and cookie cans, plastic margarine containers for the smaller flowers, tall potato chip or pretzel containers for short spike flowers, plastic shoe and sweater boxes. It is unnecessary to buy containers when all these throwaways (except shoe and sweater boxes) are at your fingertips. The only requisite for the drying container is that it be sealable and as airtight as possible.

Photo opposite: A typical Flemish design arrangement using flowers of all seasons and placed in an antique alabaster vase.

Steps in Drying with Silica Gel

Always wire the flower before drying. Trying to wire a delicate, brittle, dried stem can become very frustrating. As the stem and sepal dry, they shrink down onto the wire, securing it firmly. The glue placed on the inserted tip of the wire adds to the security of the dried stem and wire. Experience will soon teach you how far the wire must be inserted. Do not run the wire through the face of single, flat-faced flowers, especially daisies. As the flower shrinks in the drying process, any small hole from a wire will be multiplied many times over.

Spread an even layer of 1 inch to 2 inches of silica gel in the bottom of the drying container. Cut the flower stem 1 inch to 2 inches long. Dip the pointed tip of an appropriate gauge wire in Velverette glue and insert into the stem, easing it in as far as possible without splitting the stem, as shown in photo A. Allow 1 inch or more of wire to protrude from the end of the stem. Bend this protruding wire to an L shape in order to conserve on the depth of the first layer of silica gel.

A

Place the stem into the drying container with the flower petals resting on the silica gel and spaced so the individual flowers are not touching, as shown in photo B. It is best to dry only one type of flower at a time until you have mastered the timing technique for individual flowers.

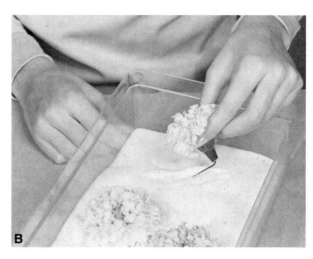
B

With a scoop or spoon, gently sprinkle silica gel over the flowers until they are completely covered, with no air pockets around or under the flower parts. See photo C.

C

Cover and seal the container. Label the container with the name of the flower, date and hour as shown in photo D. Use this for future reference in determining the necessary drying time.

D

10

The drying time will depend on the texture and moisture content of the plant material and will vary from two to five days. Overdrying tends to make the plant material very brittle and their texture and color is lost. It is best to try various drying times on different types of plant material to ascertain which is best. In a subsequent section I have listed the flowers best suited for drying, the approximate drying time in silica gel, and other information pertinent to the drying of specific species or varieties of plant materials.

To remove the dried flowers from the silica gel, slowly tip the container and carefully pour the silica gel into another container until the dried flower is fully exposed. Remove the dried flower from the container with fingers or tweezers.

With a very fine camel's hair or cosmetic brush, gently remove any small particles of the silica gel and dust.

As soon as I have all the silica gel and dust removed, I spray my dried plant materials with Flora-Set Clear or DMP (dried material preservative). Both are aerosol sprays and help retain the color and prevent shedding and shattering. Both of these sprays help retain the natural appearance of the dried material without leaving a gloss or sheen.

To store the flowers for future use, I place a small amount of silica gel in the bottom of a storage box and cover this with a sheet of tissue or soft paper. I then place my dried flowers on the tissue until I am ready to arrange them. The silica gel under the tissue will tend to absorb some of the humidity that might prevail during our Midwest springs and summer. Place this storage box, clearly labeled, in the driest area you can find.

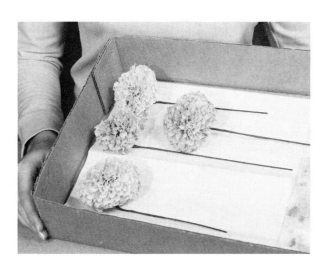

This compote is arranged with lilacs, roses, daisies and maidenhair fern which were dried in silica gel. The baby's breath was air-dried.

Dry some of the stems of the flower heads you are using. Strip the foliage from the stems and spread out in an open box to dry, turning them every few days so all sides dry to the same color and texture. The dried stems of hollow-stemmed flowers are invaluable. As soon as the flower heads are removed from the drying medium, place a bit of glue on the wire stem and insert this wire stem into the hollow dried stem. This is especially good to do with zinnias, delphinium and other hollow-stemmed flowers. For stems that are not hollow, place the base of the wired dry flower head at the top of the dried stem and secure with a binding of twig green floratape. Select a stem that resembles, as nearly as possible, the natural stem of the flower.

Cup-shaped flowers like the tulip, rose, single peonies, crocus, hollyhock and poppy to mention but a few, require special handling in the drying medium in order to retain their natural cup-like form. Sprinkle the silica gel both inside and outside of the petals simultaneously, continuing this method until there is a gradual build-up with an even level of the desiccant on both sides of the petal.

Stems of spike flowers often take a day or two longer to dry than the florets on the stems. I estimate the drying time for the florets in silica gel and complete the stem drying by hanging the flowering spikes upside down in a dry, airy, dark area for an additional day or two. This method is used especially for Spirea (bridal wreath) and other deciduous shrubs with blooms along their branches, and for delphinium, larkspur, salvia, snapdragon, stock, veronica, bells of Ireland, etc. If a form flower stem is sufficiently heavy, I oftentimes cut and dry the entire flower, stem and foliage. This requires a much larger drying container and a greater quantity of silica gel, but it is often worth the additional expenditure. Again, I gauge the drying time for the flower head and

foliage, completing the stem drying by hanging upside-down in air.

Spike flowers and form flowers with stems and foliage attached are placed on a notched cardboard tent-shaped brace that will prevent the bottom florets from being crushed and the bottom petals of the form flower from being

bent. I use my finger or the handle of my camel's hair artist's brush to shape the petals, florets and foliages as I gently sprinkle the silica gel over the flowers. This retains the natural three dimensional appearance of the flowers and foliages after they have been removed from the drying medium.

Except in the case of foliages, only the layer of flowers should be dried at one time. Foliages can be dried successfully in layers with one inch of silica gel between each layer of foliage. Treat branches of foliages from shrubs or trees the same as spike flowers, as explained in the preceding paragraph.

Drying Plant Materials in Sand

Sand is probably the oldest known drying medium, dating back to the days of the pharaohs of Egypt. It was later used by the Greeks and Romans to dry flowers and foliages for decorating the temples and the palatial homes of the wealthy. Even the homes of the humble had bouquets that had been gathered during the blooming season and dried to use when flowers were not so plentiful. Flowers, whether fresh or dried, have always played an important role in the lives of mankind.

Sand is by far the least expensive of all the drying mediums. Sand is also the slowest, taking two to four times longer than silica gel. If time is not a factor then use sand.

The best sand to use for this purpose is silica sand, sometimes labeled "glass sand" and is available at some garden centers, craft and hobby shops. Do not use sands that contain salts, clay, dirt or other impurities. Use only silica sand. The others can do more damage than good to dried material.

Sand is about the only drying medium that will not burn the color of materials left in too long. The main concern is to try not to uncover the drying plant materials too soon. If you are planning a vacation or a weekend away, you will not have to worry about your materials being over-dried or having a color burn while you are away. A few years ago I witnessed the removal of marigolds that had been in this drying medium over six months and they were beautiful—and dry!

Wire and prepare your plant material (see page 10 for instructions). The silica sand drying boxes do not have to be airtight, or even covered as in the use of silica gel. Shoe boxes or any sturdy cardboard box will do. Spread about one inch of silica sand evenly in the bottom of the drying box. Place the flowers on the layer of sand and sprinkle silica sand very slowly and carefully until the flowers or plant material is completely covered. Label the box, but do not cover. Place the drying box in a dry place where it will not be disturbed until the flowers are to be removed. Drying time for daffodils in silica gel is three days, whereas it requires about ten days in silica sand. Zinnias require three to four days in silica gel and in silica sand from ten to twenty-one days, depending on the texture and water level in the flowers. Practice is the only way you will learn to determine the amount of drying time needed for different varieties of plant materials.

This arrangement of roses, carnations, anemones, maidenhair fern, combined with bleached broom blooms is still colorful after eight years of use in my home and on my lecture tours.

Prior to the advent of the microwave oven some plant materials took several weeks for drying time. With this new type oven the drying process can be completed in a matter of hours.

Several of my garden club friends had heard of this method but had very little procedure information available. So I really started from scratch. A few hours after a phone call to one of my garden club friends she drove up to my door with an Amana Radarange to use in my experimenting. I immediately began to enjoy the recuperation from a month's hospitalization. It was just the therapy I needed and I certainly do appreciate Sandy and Michael Fleming's generosity in loaning me their oven. Now I will share with you my month's experience in this process of flower drying.

Along with the oven, one needs a supportive substance such as silica gel or the other drying agents listed previously in this section. I tried them all but found silica gel to be the best. At one time I had every oven-proof container from my cupboards filled with flowers and silica gel. My kitchen table and counters were piled high with boxes in which to store my microwave ovendried flowers.

The flowers, foliages, berries, etc. are covered with silica gel in an oven-proof container in very much the same manner as outlined in the first part of this section. Since there cannot be any metal in the microwave oven, the wiring process must be completed after the flower has dried. I suggest an inch or two of the stem be left on the flower in order to have a base for the wire that must be added to lengthen the stem.

After removing from the microwave oven, I florataped a six-inch length #30 gauge florist wire to the flower stem, then florataped a #18 gauge wire to the wired stem to support the flower head and give the added length needed for the completed design. This is a process requiring patience and skill in order that the dried flowers do not shatter. On some small flowers I dipped a six-inch length of #26 gauge milliners wire in Quick glue and placed it against the short flower stem, taping it after the glue had thoroughly dried.

Drying the Microwave Way

The flowers must be completely covered in the oven-proof container with the supportive agent. Place the container in the oven along with another small dish filled with water to provide moisture during the drying process. Set the oven at the desired timing. After the oven shuts off, remove the container from the oven and allow the flowers to remain in the agent for the allotted time. Remove flowers from the agent. With a slight tap, remove the silica gel granules and use a cosmetic or artist's fine brush to remove any additional granules or dust from the plant material. Now you are ready to add the supportive stem as outlined in the previous paragraph.

During my month-long experimentation, I dried iris, carnations, cornflowers, anemones, jonquils, tulips, hyacinths, hen and chickens, magnolia *stellata* and *soulangeana* (which turned a beige color with the timer set at 2½ minutes), ivy strands and roses. The flowers other than the magnolia were dried with the oven timer set at ranges from 2 to 3 minutes and allowed to remain in the silica gel from 8 to 12 hours. These are all approximate times as each flower has a different substance and must be treated accordingly.

My experience seems to show that 2 to 2½ minutes is ample microwave oven-drying time, with more thought given to the time the flowers are left in the silica gel after removing from the oven.

Again a few simple rules: only those flowers at the peak of their bloom should be used. Flowers must not have any dew or moisture on the petals. Flowers or foliages should not be crowded with petals or leaves touching each other.

If you are fortunate in having the use of a microwave oven, you will find a new and fresh approach to flower drying. And I assure you it has been a fascinating and rewarding experience for me!

Cornmeal is sometimes added to the silica sand in order to lighten the weight; but the cornmeal often attracts bugs and does little or nothing that silica sand cannot do alone.

Borax combined with sand will burn the colors when left in too long and needs very close attention.

Kitty litter is a newcomer to the drying market. The only favorable results I have had were with leatherleaf fern, rose foliage, and mahonia leaves. It was not satisfactory for drying any of the flowering materials, as they wilted faster than the litter could absorb the moisture content and were shriveled and drab in color when removed from the drying box.

"Cherish" Drying Medium

Although I have not been too well pleased in my early experiments with this new organic drying material marketed under the trade name Cherish, I feel it warrants mention and space in this book, especially for those willing to try new substitute products. I had satisfactory results in drying strands of ivy, mahonia, fern leaves, cotoneaster, blooming forsythia branches and foliages from deciduous trees. Most flowers that I used in this experiment lost their luminosity and radiance; however, they do dry without the usual brittleness compared to those in other drying mediums.

A much lower cost is one factor in favor of this drying agent. Too, it is very lightweight and easy to handle. An equal weight of Cherish dries twice as many flowers as silica gel. The drying containers cannot be sealed, thereby permitting the use of any ordinary household container.

The preliminary preparation and placement of the flowers prior to embedding in Cherish is the same as I outlined in the previous pages under "Silica gel." A very complete instruction brochure accompanies each container of Cherish. Read and study thoroughly before using.

Cherish should be available in florist shops, garden centers or craft shops.

The antique silver coffeepot contains delphinium and Queen Anne's lace, both dried in silica gel.

Comments on Other Desiccants

An old brown crock is filled with dried wild ball mustard, foxtail grass, teasels, contrived hedge apple flowers and preserved goldenrod.

Air Drying

Air drying is by far the easiest and least expensive method of plant drying. So many of our summer and autumn plant materials prefer this method, rather than being embedded in a drying medium. Conditions must be just right for harvesting material to be air dried. It is best to gather materials on a dry day, preferably after the sun has dried off the morning dew. Many times, however, regardless of weather conditions, you will have to gather your plant materials when you can.

Harvesting starts in the spring when the small seed capsules of the tiny spring flowers are ready for gathering. From then on, each week and month brings forth new materials that are ready for harvest, even through the cold winter months. Hardly a week goes by throughout the entire year that I am not bringing in seed heads, grains, branches or other materials that I have found in my garden, in hedgerows, along fences or country roadsides.

Generally speaking, seed heads, grains and grasses dry naturally; however, it is sometimes safer to bring them inside to dry under more controlled conditions.

Cut the stems to the desired lengths, keeping in mind what you will need when making the completed designs. Remove the foliage and any unnecessary side shoots or damaged parts. It is not necessary to remove all the foliage. However, I find the drying process is hastened and the materials are more apt to retain their natural color if about 90% of the foliage is removed before starting the drying process.

Air drying is divided into two methods:

Hang Dry

To hang dry, tie the plant material in small bunches, allowing ample space between the heads and stems for air circulation. I use whatever taping material is available—plasties, twistems, twine, florataped wire or rubber bands—all bindings that will not cut into the stems. I prefer rubber bands as they generally hold the stems together in bunches through the drying process. Rubber bands stretched tightly around the base of the stems will hold the bunches securely, as the stems shrink during this drying. A wire with a hook at each end can be used to hang the bunches. Insert one end of the hooked wire through the rubber bands and the opposite hook to either a nail in the garage rafters, over a stretched wire or a rope line or suspended wire coat hanger.

Hang the bunches in a dark airy place, such as a garage, attic or storeroom. (The cross rafters of my garage are always loaded with dried materials.) After they are thoroughly dried, spray with a moisture barrier spray. Store in boxes or place in pliofilm bags and rehang on the rafters until ready for use.

Stand Dry

Many of my plant materials respond better to the stand dry method of drying, and I find it convenient when I run out of rafter space. For this method I use a container with about an inch of room-temperature water, cutting each stem before placing into the container. Be sure the stem ends reach to the bottom of the container and are not crowded. Again, allow for sufficient air circulation through the stems and flower heads. Do not add any additional water. When all are completely dry, spray and store as I described in the previous paragraph.

Some of the delicate stem grasses can be dried flat on trays, box lids or even loose on shelves or cupboard tops. The same applies to many of the spike seed heads.

In their catalogs many seed companies are now listing under separate headings the varieties of annuals and perennials that are recommended for drying.

Don't stop with the varieties I have listed. Open your eyes and see the beauty in the many forms of nature that lie at your very fingertips—stems, flowers, foliages, seed heads, branches, gnarled roots, barks, lichens. Be aware!

I have had favorable results in the air-dry process with the plant materials listed below:

ACHILLEA or YARROW. Hang or stand dry. Pick when flowers are just beginning to open as they will develop more fully as they dry.

ALLIUMS (onions, garlics, chives). Stand dry the garlic blooms and hang dry the onions and chives.

BABY'S BREATH (Gypsophila). The Bristol Fairy and Perfecta varieties of the hardy type are the best to grow for drying. Cut sprays as soon as they start to show their tiny white flowers. Stand dry for best results. If they become too matted after drying, dip entire spray in hot water for a few minutes. This will soften them and they can be pulled apart and fluffed out without too much damage to the flowers and stems.

BELLS OF IRELAND. Use either hang or stand dry process.

BURDOCK. Cut at various stages of coloration and hang dry.

CHINESE LANTERNS. Cut when the lanterns have not fully ripened to the top. Hang or stand dry.

CLEMATIS, especially the variety texensis. These fluffy seed heads should be picked soon after they turn green and are best hang dried.

COLUMBINE. Cut the seed heads as soon as they open and start forming an outward curve. Hang dry.

DELPHINIUM and LARKSPUR. If you missed drying the blooms in a dessicant, watch for the seed heads. Dry flat or by hanging.

DOCK. Gather these at various stages from the pale green through the rich brown red. Cutting some each week will give you a wide range of colorations. Hang dry, stand dry or flat dry. If you want interesting curves, lay in a box much shorter than the length of the stem and bend to fit in the box. Place one next to the other but do not layer.

FOXGLOVE. The spike seed heads form an interesting pattern. Stand or hang.

GLOBE THISTLE. Cut these in the early stage just as they are beginning to open. Stand dry.

GOLDENROD. Select as soon as they show color as they will open as they mature and dry. Allow the side shoots to remain on the main stem and remove these laterals after drying. Stand or hang.

GRAINS and GRASSES. Cut at various stages and they will dry from a pale green to a light beige color. Depending on the stem strength, these can be dried flat, hanging or standing.

HOLLYHOCK. One year I missed the blooms and dried the stems with the seed pods. Stand dry.

HONESTY, HONEST PETER'S PENNY, MONEY PLANT (Lunaria). These have always given me trouble. After hang drying, remove the brown outer layer of skin to expose the silvery tissue-like seedpods.

LAVENDER. Cut these before the flowers are fully open, and they will develop and dry in the stand dry process.

LUPINES. My sister has five clumps of this hardy perennial in her garden, providing a bright splash of color and ample seed heads for dried arrangements. The seed heads on the spike are similar to dried pea pods.

POPPIES. The seed heads of all the poppies are invaluable to the flower arranger. Allow them to dry on the plant and scatter seeds for a crop the following season. Stand dry after cutting.

STATICE. All varieties of statice are best dried by using the stand dry method.

SMOKE TREE (Cotinus). Stand dry the fluffy, smoke-like seed heads of this small tree.

SUMAC (Rhus). This common shrub is a riot of color in the fall, ranging from red orange to dark mahogany red. Cut the seed heads at their peak of brilliancy to retain their color. Remove all leaves and hang dry.

TEASEL. These grow wild in the poorest soil and in some areas are considered obnoxious. Gather in various stages for varied colorations.

STRAWFLOWERS, GLOBE AMARANTH, ACRO-CLINIUM (Everlastings) are all annuals that provide excellent color for the arranger. Cut as soon as these flowers reach the peak of their perfection and hang dry.

The preservation of foliages, berries and certain varieties of flowers and evergreens provides the arranger with a wealth of beautiful materials.

The method is relatively simple. Branches should be cut when they are mature and have slowed or stopped their annual growth. In the Midwest this usually ranges from mid-August to mid-September, depending entirely on climatic conditions and the variety of plant material. Cut the branches with not more than three years' growth, remembering that the heavier the stem the slower the absorption. This yearly growth can be noted by the change of color and texture on the branch. The lighter, smoother shades indicate the latest growth, varying down the stem to a deeper color with heavier texture. Most branches of deciduous trees and shrubs will show a very definite ring that separates the seasonal growth.

Select branches with clean unblemished foliage and remove about three or four inches of the lower leaves. To help accelerate the absorption process, I generally allow the branches to lie on my worktable for an hour or two after cutting so they lose some of their turgidity. They are then thirsty and draw the solution more rapidly.

Cut one inch from the stem and crush end with a blunt instrument. This loosens the fibers and accelerates the capillary action in absorbing the solution. Immediately, place these freshly cut and crushed stems in a solution of one part glycerine to two parts warm water. Temperature of water can vary with the degree of texture of the stem. For delicately textured branches use lukewarm water; for a heavy, woody texture use hot water. There should be about 6 inches of solution in the container.

Keep in a light airy room (not sunny) until tiny beads of moisture appear on the upper-most leaves. When these appear it is time to remove the branch or branches from the solution. Hang branches upside-down until the leaves show a change from the natural green to russet, black, dark green or brown. By this time the tiny beads will have disappeared.

Preserving Plant Materials in Glycerine

Cover any items that might be under the hanging branches as the solution will drip and might stain. I recall my early experience in hanging them from the garage rafters over the area where the car was parked. My brother-in-law Clarence was in the service station business at that time and took my white station wagon to be serviced and washed. He was sure that we had a new breed of birds roosting in our garage. So beware.

Absorption time will vary according to the variety of plant material, existing growing conditions and moisture content. Seldom will two identical branches complete the absorption process at the same time. I allow a minimum of ten days to two weeks for absorption, but some varieties will take up to six weeks for complete absorption. After they have been in the solution for a week or ten days, start daily examination to determine if they are ready for removal.

Keep watching the solution level and if necessary add additional room temperature solution to the container. I usually start with four to six inches of solution in the container and try to maintain this level throughout the process.

When all materials have been glycerinized, I save the solution by straining and storing in a jar for later use. When reusing, shake or stir the solution and strain again into a pan and reheat to the necessary temperature. The heated solution speeds the absorption process into the cells of the freshly cut plant material.

Vines, such as ivy or euonymus, some varieties of ferns, as well as individual leaves of trees and shrubs can be preserved by immersion. Prepare the same proportion of glycerine and room temperature water. Immerse the foliages and weight down to keep them from floating. Allow the materials to soak until they are thoroughly preserved. This immersion process will take from three to five days, depending entirely on the condition of the plant material. Remove from the solution and allow to drip-dry, then immerse in a warm sudsy water solution, rinse in clear water and allow to cure by placing materials on shallow boxes or box lids which have layers of newspapers for absorption.

This same process can be used to preserve leaves that are changing to autumn colors. These colored leaves must have a moisture content before immersing. They cannot be crisp or brittle. Immerse, weight them down and allow them to stay immersed about three or four days. Remove, drip-dry, wash, rinse and cure as before.

Whenever glycerinized foliages become dry or brittle, immerse in hot water for a few minutes and allow to drip-dry. Oftentimes this treatment brings out the solution stored in the veins of the foliage and the flexibility is regained. They will, however, only respond to one or two such treatments.

If you are preserving a quantity of plant material it would be best to purchase glycerine in a 10 or 12 pound can. Druggists can order this for you, and it is much more economical than buying the small bottles.

I have successfully preserved the following list of plant materials:

ARBORVITAE (THUJA). I have had success with both methods—immersing the short sprays and standing the longer branches. After shearing my arborvitae trees I gather the small sprays for immersion. This is valuable material for a backing and filler in wreaths of dried material, and can be cut anytime, even during the cold winter months.

ASPIDISTRA (IRON PLANT). Took nearly 4 months for stem absorption, 3 weeks for the immersion method, but was worth the time.

BEECH. The copper beech cures to a beautiful glowing copper brown.

BELLS OF IRELAND. Turn brownish green but will lighten considerably if placed in a sunny place for a couple of weeks.

BLACKBERRIES and RASPBERRIES. Thorny but worth it. Pick short branches with leaves and berries.

BUCKEYE (HORSE CHESTNUT). Immerse or stand the individual leaf stems. It changes from the green to a very rich brown.

COTONEASTER. All varieties turn a rich brown. Every landscape should include some variety of this worthwhile shrub.

DOCK. Start with the green seed heads and put some in solution each week through the entire season. The dark reddish brown varieties are strikingly beautiful.

EUCALYPTUS. I buy this fresh from a florist before it has been put in water. Turns to shades of dark green through light brown.

EUONYMUS. The evergreen varieties *fortunei* and especially the *radicans vegetus* variety (Evergreen Bittersweet) preserve well by either immersing or standing. The berries are often reluctant to hang to the vine. The deciduous variety, *alatus* (cork bark), turns a rich tone of plum brown. Use the hot solution on this variety and select stems with not more than two year's growth.

HOLLY. (*Ilex* varieties). Berries will shrivel but have an interesting texture.

HYDRANGEA. Both varieties, *arborescens* (Hills of Snow) and *paniculata grandiflora* (Pee Gee) are easy to preserve. Cut the *arborescens* variety after it has started to mature into its second green color. This variety is first green, then white and as it matures changes again to a pale green before it turns beige and then into tan and browns. Cut some at each stage of coloration to provide various shades in your arrangements. Cut the Pee Gee variety after it passes the rosy color and starts maturing to a light tan color. Hot solution is best for the Pee Gee variety as it generally has a very woody stem.

IVY. Sprays or individual leaves can be best preserved by the immersion method.

Preserved dock, goldenrod, beech foliage and hydrangeas are arranged in a low stoneware bowl.

JUNIPER. The *canaerti* variety is my pet. These lovely and graceful branches loaded with the blue berries are a welcome addition to the arranger's source of material. Stem absorption in very warm solution.

LAUREL. Leaves turn very dark.

MAGNOLIA. I have not had success with the *soulangeana* or *stellata* varieties. However the Southern *grandiflora* variety preserves very well. Individual leaves can be immersed. Branches should be placed in hot solution due to the very woody stems. Final colorations will vary from very dark green, almost black, to rich brown.

MAHONIA (Oregon Holly Grape). Individual leaf sprays and branches can be preserved by stem absorption or the leaf sprays can be immersed.

MAPLE. Single leaves can be immersed while short one or two year branches can be placed upright for stem absorption.

MOUNTAIN ASH. The sprays of leaves and berries preserve beautifully. Cut branches while berries are green as they mature to an orange while in the solution. Spray the berries with a moisture barrier after removing from solution and prior to curing.

OAK. The pin oak changes to a rich dark green and then to brown. Branches of the pin oak can be cut longer and preserve well whereas other varieties have a slower growth habit and very woody stems. For these very woody stemmed varieties, increase the temperature of the solution to hot. Cut some branches with acorns as they preserve and hold well to the stem. Individual leaves can be immersed.

PEAR and APPLE. I trim the "water sprouts" that grow on the main trunk between the branches. Hot solution is best. Turns a rich brown color. Small green pears will shrivel but preserve well and hold to the branch. I have not successfully preserved the apples on the branch.

PEONY. Stems of the peony foliage preserve very well and finish off with a two-tone effect.

PYRACANTHA. All varieties of this berried shrub preserve well. I suggest spraying the berries or fruit with a moisture barrier spray after removing from the solution. It will not prevent shriveling, but it helps retain their form.

RHODODENDRON. Preserved some branches years ago and they remained a beautiful dark green for several years. The tight buds at the top were shades lighter than the foliage and made an interesting contrast. The leaves had a tendency to curl but the contrast is great when used with heavier foliages. These, like oak, require a hot solution.

ROSE. I have cut the branches of the old-fashioned briar roses and they preserved well when I increased the temperature of the solution. The sprays of rose-hips on the multiflora rose preserve well and deserve a spray with a moisture barrier before the final curing. If you want to retain their natural gloss, spray with Gard's Clear Porcelain spray. This same type spray material applies to all berried branches.

ROSEMARY. I have never tried this but saw some that was preserved and had retained its lovely silver-gray color and scent. Have ordered several plants from an herbist for this year's garden.

SYCAMORE. Immerse the large leaves.

TULIP TREE *(Liriodendron)*. I have been successful in using the immersion method only for individual leaves. Somehow I have not been able to have the branches absorb the solution faster than wilting and drying occurs. These individual leaves present an interesting contrast when used in arrangements and especially so in wreaths of dried materials.

VIBURNUM. All varieties of this popular shrub preserve well. I am especially fond of the variety *lantanaphyllum* with its heavy rich brown foliage; *seiboldiana* is another good variety. The foliage of *americanum* (Highbush Cranberry) changes to a rich deep brown; however, the berries do not mature well.

I have successfully preserved the varieties listed here. There are many more varieties available for experimentation. If your first attempt fails, test at various stages of the plant maturity and with different degrees of solution temperature. It is always a challenge to experiment until one is completely successful.

Now I have completed the discussion and the mechanics involved in the various processes of drying and preserving plant material. The following sections of this book will be devoted to the mechanics and details involved in arranging several specific varieties of plant materials.

I encourage you to develop your own methods, merely using my notes as a guideline. There will be failures but do not despair for then all the joy and fun is lost.

Too, I cannot overemphasize that you constantly keep your eyes open and discover new and different plant materials to dry, to preserve, to press. Many times you will find these right at your doorstep. I'm repeating again the admonishment of Mrs. Myrtle Walgreen, widow of the founder of the Walgreen drug chain. As we were walking through the gardens at Hazelwood, their Dixon, Illinois, estate, I neglected to notice one of her choice blooms. She said, "Too many look but never see." I began to "see." I hope it becomes contagious and spreads to you and you and you!

Here are some suggestions for prolonging the enjoyment of all dried plant materials:

1. Be sure the moisture content has been completely removed from flower, stem and foliage before using in completed design. This applies to those dried in a dessicant, pressed or hang (air) dried.

2. Spraying with an aerosol preservative helps to prevent shedding and shattering, retains natural color and prevents fading, and in some instances retards unpleasant odors. Sprays under the trade names of "DMP" (Dried materials preservatives); Floraset Clear or "Cherish" should be available at florists, garden centers or craft shops. Read and carefully follow the directions on the label.

3. Humidity is another enemy of dried flowers, especially the spring and early summer varieties. Store or display in a dry area.

4. Keep from intense light or sunlight to prevent fading.

5. Place out of reach of inquisitive fingers.

Lilacs, roses, carnations, baby's breath and maidenhair fern are arranged in a shallow, cut-crystal bowl. Vase arrangement of twelve peppermint carnations are combined with baby's breath and maidenhair fern.

It has been great fun drying and preserving the plant materials, and now we will have the joy of arranging them. And a joy it is, especially when one has the few necessary tools and supplies available to work with plus some knowledge of the principles of design. Flower arranging should be a pleasure and a joy, yet I have watched so many who seemed terrified and frustrated while arranging. Always remember that you are arranging form and color to create a design that is pleasing to you. Learn all the rules of good design—then break them and enjoy the art of arranging! Unknown to you, these rules will somehow dominate you; and each successive design will show improvement. Read and study good books on flower arranging, and learn the elements of design: scale and proportion, line, color, texture, pattern and form. You will soon discover what an easy yet rewarding experience may be found in flower arranging. Lose all that tension and frustration and just enjoy it!

I cannot overemphasize the necessity of starting with a knowledge of good mechanics. And number one on my list is having the proper holder firmly secured to a suitable container or base.

Holders

For dried and preserved arrangements, I recommend three foam holders: Styrofoam; dry foam such as "Fill-Fast" or "Oasis"; and "Bar-Fast." Styrofoam is an especially suitable base for heavy and sturdy stemmed plant materials or delicate stems that are bound together with wood or metal florist picks. The dry foams will generally accept the most delicate stems without using the picks, however the heavy-stemmed plant materials have a tendency to become loose and do not stay in position in the dry foam bases.

One of my favorite bases for dried materials is "Bar-Fast," a relative newcomer to the market and manufactured exclusively for use in arranging dried flowers. "Bar-Fast" is a moist foam containing a secret formula that

The Mechanics of Flower Arranging

locks the stems in place and holds them firmly after the foam becomes dry, which generally takes about twenty-four hours. The most delicate stems penetrate this moist foam and the heavy stems remain in position without the addition of wires or picks. After it has dried, only picked or heavy pointed natural stems can be forced into the foam, so the arranger must complete the design while the foam is still moist.

Styrofoam is secured to a container by placing a narrow band of florist clay (I prefer Cling) around the base, pressing it firmly into the container with a clockwise turn. I usually camouflage the green Styrofoam by covering with sheet moss, securing the moss to the

Right: Dried yellow yarrow is arranged in a basket with dock, goldenrod and other roadside materials.

Left: An old brown crock is filled with dried wild ball mustard, foxtail grass, teasels, contrived hedge apple flowers and preserved goldenrod. The wall hanging is made of spices depicting trees of the four seasons and was made by Lynn McCleary, a friend who teaches the fourth grade at Sugar Grove, Illinois.

Basic supplies necessary for flower arrangements including florist tape, Styrofoam, dried Oasis (Sahara could be used) and foam cut to fit snugly in a cylindrical vase and glue.

For vases or cylinders, I recommend cutting the Styrofoam or other foam to fit snuggly within the top of the container. Fill heavy-based vases with lightweight mica insulation pellets; fill a lightweight vase with clean dry sand. Allow the foam holder to rest on the filler material, with the holder extending one to two inches above the rim of the vase. Secure the foam holder with tape and the Styrofoam with Cling as described in the above paragraphs.

When using this type container I prefer using the Styrofoam holder. The delicate stems that will not penetrate the moss-covered Styrofoam holder should be bound to a wooden florist pick before inserting. Cut the heavy stems at a sharp angle or point and place a small band of floral clay around the stem about an inch from the end, or dip the stem end into glue before inserting it in the Styrofoam base. This will hold the heavy stems in position. The wood picks have a rough surface that will secure to Styrofoam without the use of an adhesive.

Another method of securing the foam holders to low containers is to use a needle-point holder firmly secured to the container with Cling, then impale the foam on the points. I suggest you use a small piece of nylon hosiery at the base of the foam before placing it on the needle points. This will allow for easy removal from the points and is a timesaver when trying to clean the foam from the areas between the needle points.

Picks

If it becomes necessary to pick the materials into the holder, we generally use the wired florist picks which are available in 2½-inch, 3-inch, 4-inch and 6-inch lengths. Hold a single stem or clusters of smaller stems firmly against the wired florist pick, allowing one inch or more of the stems to be bound to the pick. Bind attached wire firmly around stems only, above top of pick. Then proceed with the wire, binding stems and picks, spiraling towards end

Styrofoam with florist greening pins. To remove Styrofoam from container grasp Styrofoam firmly, turn counter clockwise and lift from the container. Use household cooking oil to remove any traces of Cling from the container.

The other foam materials can be secured to the container by a narrow strip of florist waterproof adhesive tape placed across the top of the block and adhered to the top sides of the container. The foam should be cut to allow the holder to extend an inch or two above the rim of the container, thus enabling the stems of the plant material to be placed at angles in the arrangement.

of stems with last two binds on pick only. The photos show details of this very important mechanical step.

Balance

Determine the height and width of the design by using a good and pleasing proportion for the space the arrangement will occupy. The beginner might want to use the old rule that an arrangement should be at least one and one-half times the height of the container, or one and one-half times the width of the low containers, bowls, bases, etc. Most experts in floral design agree that this proportion can be up to three times the width or height of the container if light, delicate or airy material is used for the height. A balance is maintained by the placement of heavier textured material at the base. Always strive for good proportion in all of your designs.

Line, color, texture, pattern and form are the elements of design. We generally begin the design by selecting and using the line or spike flowers, placing these in the arrangements to form the desired shape or outline. The form or round flowers are then placed in the design, following later with the foliage or filler.

Always remember to place the spike flowers to the top and sides of the arrangement with the form flowers to the center and base of the design. The same is true of color placement, using the lighter colors to the top and outside with the deeper colors towards the center and base. Follow these simple rules and you will be off to a good start.

Pattern

The pattern in your arrangement should have a feeling of rhythm. This is often determined by the position of the solid flowers, keeping in mind the space or voids that should be thoughtfully planned with the placement of each flower. To achieve good rhythm, use a repetition of the elements to create a pattern of flow and movement. This is achieved by a repetition of line and line directions, of colors, shapes, sizes and texture of the elements you are using in the design. One aspect or combination should become dominant such as the brilliance or unusual texture of a flower, foliage, pod, or other material used. This will exert a dominant influence in the design.

Texture

Texture is a very important element of design. A slight change or twist in the placement of a form flower often adds a great deal of interest to the overall texture and pattern of the design. Foliages or branches with a strong silhouette add interesting patterns and texture to the completed arrangement. Place some of the larger form flowers deep into the arrangement with longer stemmed smaller form flowers extending over and above. When the design is completed, all the flower stems should appear to be radiating from one central position—very much like the stems of clumps of flowers growing in your garden.

For the beginner, I suggest you collect a series of pictures of good flower arrangements and use these as patterns until you have achieved a feeling of self-assurance and satisfaction. There are many fine books in stores and libraries that are available to those interested in becoming more knowledgeable in this field.

In my lectures and classes I have always insisted that good mechanics come first. Study the placement of line, color, texture, pattern and form. Soon these all meld and you are on your way to happy flower arranging!

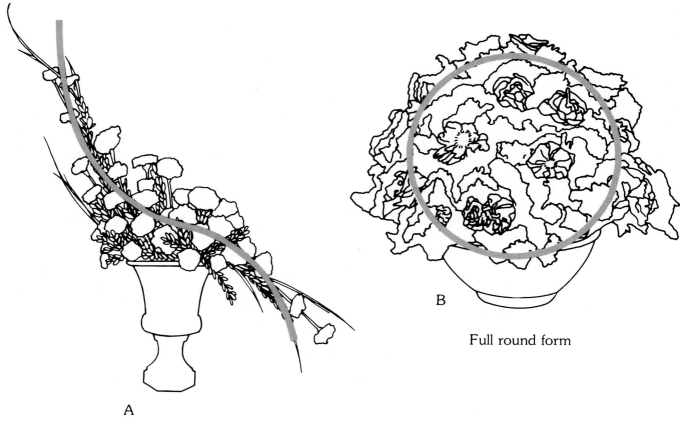

A

Hogarth or *S* curve

Full round form

B

C

Triangle

Form

The form of the flowers and plant materials in the arrangement can be based on several familiar geometric figures. For instance, the Hogarth or *S* curve (A) is a graceful form which lends itself to a tall and classic vase, as shown in the diagram. This curve is often called "the line of beauty" and is especially effective when used in vases or compotes.

The full, round form (B), so reminiscent of the typical Colonial Williamsburg arrangement, has always been one of our standards in flower designs.

A floral arrangement based on the triangle (C) is a meaningful form when used in altar arrangements.

Photo opposite: Arrangements utilizing the triangle, the full round form and the right triangle.

Variations of the triangle (D and G) lend themselves to various containers. The elongated triangle is suited to taller vases; and an arrangement based on a right triangle is suitable for a flatter vase and makes for a striking form.

The crescent shape (F) and the circle (B) are especially suitable forms for arrangements in the Oriental manner. A modified *S* curve (E) is an especially graceful arrangement in a low bowl or compote.

Above: These are two examples of dried arrangements which use purchased materials. The design on top is a contemporary one of lotus pods and bleached soya arranged in a reproduction of an early Egyptian container. Standing below is a modern low pottery bowl filled with bleached cordones, mountain fern, white lagurus and reed swirls.

Right, from top to bottom: A cut-glass cream pitcher contains miniature carnations and blooms from the graceful, early-blooming Deutzia Gracilis. Small peonies, lilacs, daisies and Artemisia "Silver King" lend charm to an old cut-glass sugar bowl. The small antique cup and saucer is filled with miniature rosebuds, baby's breath and perennial blue salvia.

D

Elongated triangle

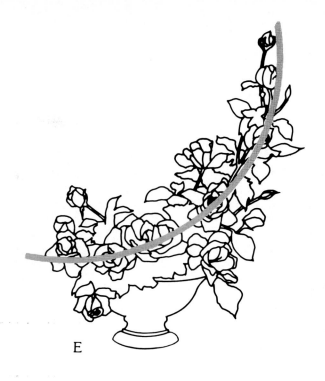

E

Modified *S* curve

F

Crescent

G

Right triangle

Dried Arrangements in Glass Domes

Two enemies of dried flowers are humidity and inquisitive fingers, both of which are more or less conquered when the arrangements are placed under glass domes. In this way, even the most fragile arrangements can be enjoyed year round.

The glass domes are reminiscent of Victorian days when flowers were made from beads, yarn, shells and wax. Even human hair was saved and woven into flowers to be placed under glass for preservation.

A dried flower arrangement under a glass dome carries a certain sentimental image whether it is a miniature in a small dome or a large design in one of the massive domes.

Glass containers need not be limited to domes. Arrangements are equally effective if placed in covered crystal candy jars, bottles, cylinders or hurricane shades. Rectangular glass containers or clear plastic boxes may also be used to protect the flowers. And for the

"swinging set" there are many interesting crystal containers that may be placed in macrame hangers.

I use a small piece of foam (Filfast, Quickee or Oasis) about 1½ inches thick, the diameter in proportion to the base of the dome. Glue the foam to the dome base and glue bits of sheet moss to the top and sides of the foam disk. The moss will cover the parts of the foam that might be difficult to cover with flowers or foliage. Dip the stem ends in glue and insert in the moss-covered foam disk.

Place the tallest materials on the base first, checking the height so the flowers do not touch the top of the dome. After the tall materials have been placed on the base, proceed on down the design to the center and then the lower section and the base. You might want to check the width and height of the arrangement periodically by placing the dome over the flowers.

Follow the same principles of design that I previously mentioned by positioning light, airy materials on the outer perimeter and the darker, heavier materials in the center and at the base of the arrangement.

Individual florets of delphinium, when wired with #26 florist wire and bound with floral tape, make excellent small flowers to use towards the center of the arrangement in order to add depth to the design.

Arranging dried materials in covered jars often requires a great deal of patience, especially when the jar's top opening is much smaller than the mid diameter. The mechanics of arranging are the same, however, in designing arrangements in other-than-usual containers. Develop your own special techniques.

A small piece of foam is glued to the dome base. Stem ends are glued and inserted into the foam, beginning with the tallest plant materials.

Wall Hangings and Plaques

Decorative wall hangings are designed using materials that have been air dried. Thus, fragile plant materials that might have a tendency to wilt when exposed to humidity are eliminated. Added to the air-dried flowers are cones, fruits, pods, seeds, vines, shells, driftings and other interesting collected materials.

When using a velvet or polished wood background, select your finest, most elegant materials. Barn boards or burlap backgrounds require heavier textured dried materials. The length and width should be in pleasing proportion to the wall area; and the materials used in the design should be in scale both with one another and with the background.

Again a reminder, follow the generally accepted principles of design by using the lighter colored and more delicate textured materials to the top and sides, with the darker colored, heavier textured materials to the center and base. Strive to have one dominant color, form and texture. Then add more interest and vigor to the design with contrasting form and textured material.

All the designs I have shown are secured to the backgrounds with either white Quik glue or with hot glue from my electric glue gun. This last method is especially satisfactory when using heavy materials.

I sometimes prearrange the material on the background or make a sketch of the design; but more often, I just sort out the material I want to use and design with a glue-as-I-work procedure. Develop the technique that is best for you.

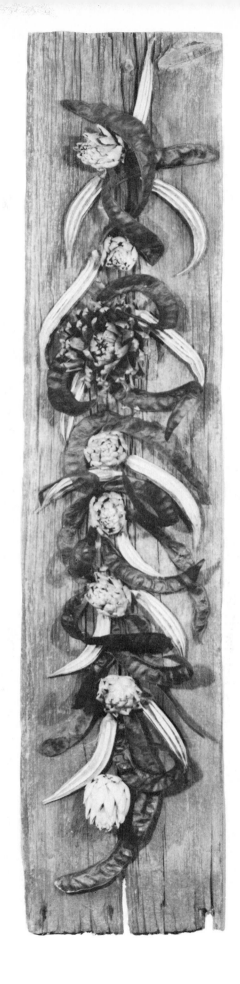

Okra, artichokes and pods from the honey locust tree were arranged on an old barn board to create an unusual contemporary arrangement for a wall plaque. The materials were secured to the board with a hot glue gun.

Designs with an Oriental Influence

So many of our natural materials with line and form lend themselves to interesting Oriental-type arrangements. The spiral branches of the corkscrew willow, the flat contorted branches of the fantail willow, the cork-like bark of the *euonymus alatus*, and the severe straight lines of the dried cornstalks are but a few of the many materials that will make interesting lines, forms or silhouettes. One particularly interesting contorted shrub that provides me with a good supply of material is "Harry Lauder's Walking Stick" (*Corylus avellana* "contorta"). Portions of grape roots from an old vineyard; gnarled sections of ancient, uprooted trees; weathered branches from a forgotten orchard; sections of tangled and twisted vines along an overgrown hedgerow; interesting forms of lichen from the base of a fallen tree; shells, driftwood and gatherings from the shoreline; interesting stones and ledge rock—well, there's just no limit to the materials that are available if we would but open our eyes and see.

I'm showing designs using just a few of the materials I've listed. The materials used are described with each arrangement. Refer to pages 27-33 for the mechanics involved in designing these arrangements.

Left: Seed heads of Goat's Beard are combined with bare branches of Harry Lauder's Walking Stick (Corylus contorta) and southern Cecropia leaves to create a striking effect in this very Oriental influenced contemporary vase.

Right: Dried and preserved materials are combined to create an Oriental design in the handsome Japanese cylinder vase, using Japanese Fantail Willow, spiral cones, Protea blooms and preserved Canaert juniper.

Pressing Plant Materials

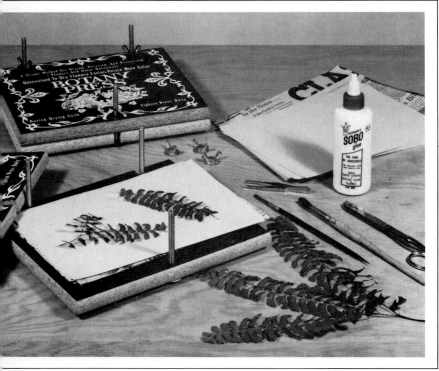

A Botany Press and specimens being pressed between processed drying paper.

This is another primitive art which has been revived during the past few years, probably the result of the universal interest in ecology and preservation of the beauty of nature.

The pressing of plant material is a relatively simple procedure, involving the use of paper as an absorbent and weights or pressure to keep the material secure until it is dried and flat. The old Sears and Montgomery Wards catalogs, if available, as well as the heavy telephone directories are excellent for pressing materials. In addition, a heavy weight should always be placed on them to speed the pressing process.

Several years ago I purchased a Botany Press and find it invaluable. I carry it with me on trips to press the flowers and foliages I find along the way or in my friend's gardens. This press is made of two fiberboards drilled with holes in which screws with wing nuts are placed. I could have made a homemade press; however, by the time I assembled all the materials, plus the time involved, the purchase of one ready-to-use was better for me. Besides, I'm not too handy with saws, hammers, drills and such tools of the carpenter trade.

The procedure in the use of the Botany Press is simple:

1. Place 10 sheets of newspaper cut to the size of the press on the bottom half of the press.

2. Add 2 sheets of drying paper and arrange a layer of your plant material on top. I use a special processed drying paper that provides fast drying and good color retention. It is manufactured especially for use with the Botany Press. As a substitute one could use facial tissue, paper towels or the like.

3. Use only one type of specimen on each layer in order to keep your press level. Do not allow petals to overlap or even touch as they will tear when they are removed from the press after being dried.

4. Cover specimens with 2 sheets of processed drying paper. The top sheet can be used to date and name the specimens for future reference.

5. Add an additional 10 sheets of pre-cut newspaper to complete the layer. There should always be 10 sheets of newspapers at the top and bottom of the press and 10 sheets between each layer of specimens.

6. When all flowers have been layered, set top on press and hand tighten wing nuts as tightly as possible.

7. Be sure to tighten press every day. Your flowers should be dry and ready in one week.

The principle involved in this type of press is to speed the drying process in order to give the best possible color retention. Some papers have a very high chemical content that tends to draw the color out of the flower during the press-dry process.

Additional layers of flowers can be added from time to time, with the lower layers remaining in the press. This is an advantage if the press is used on an extended vacation.

When ready to remove the specimens from the press, lift the two layers of drying paper with the pressed flowers between them and store in boxes until ready for use. Sprinkle some dessicant in the bottom of the storage carton to absorb any humidity that might be present. Mothballs or flakes will discourage any hungry insects or vermin. The special processed drying paper can be reused several times until the special absorption qualities are lost.

A word of warning—thick, pulpy flowers with a hard calyx oftentimes do not press well. It is sometimes necessary to slit the calyx before pressing. The same is true of heavy-stemmed flowers. It is better to cut the blooms at the stems and press the blooms on one layer and the stems on another. Spike flowers, such as the delphinium, press better if the individual florets are pressed on a separate layer and the stems, with the top buds intact, pressed on another layer. In creating a large floral picture, the florets can be glued to the dried pressed stem.

To create botanical pictures be sure to press all parts of the specimen in all its stages of development: roots, foliage, stems, buds, flowers, seeds, fruit, etc. The roots, of course, should be washed and dried before placing in the press. Only smaller fruits and pods will press; these should be dissected so as to show both the interior and exterior.

The materials are now pressed, dried and stored. Perhaps there are floral momentos of a vacation, a day's visit with friends, a wedding or a very special party. We are now ready to create a floral portrait

Materials needed to create a pressed flower "portrait": pressed plant materials, frame and glass, backing, scissors and glue.

Pressed Flower Portraits

When these lovely pressed flower portraits are given as gifts, they are certain to find prominent wall space and will soon become almost heirlooms.

A proper frame for the flower portrait is very important. I prefer a very simple frame, as one which is more ornate will detract and lessen the importance of the flowers used in the completed picture. The size and form of the flowers pressed will dictate the size and shape of the frame you select.

The background fabric for mounting the flowers should have a minimum of texture and a soft, muted coloring that will be flattering to the flowers. Velvet, linen, cotton, even some woolens make good backgrounds. Be cautious when using shiny materials such as silk or taffeta.

Cut a cardboard background to fit the frame and cover with the selected background material. This material can be secured to the cardboard with a small amount of Quik glue. Cut out a second cardboard; and arrange the plant material on it before placing the design on the background fabric. Work in a room where air circulation is at a minimum, as these pressed materials are very light and delicate.

Follow the same design principles as outlined in previous chapters. Both scale and proportion should be carefully watched. Do not allow stems to overlap, cutting away any overlapping stems to reduce bulk. Place some flowers in profile and others full-faced. Place the largest flowers and those with the brightest hues near the center of interest in the picture.

After the design planning is completed, the flowers can then be transferred to the permanent background. With tweezers, carefully lift the pressed materials. With a glue-tipped toothpick, put a tiny bit of glue on the underside of the plant material before placing it on the fabric background. When the design is completed and the glue has dried, place the clean cover glass in position. Fit the frame over the glass. Turn the picture over, holding it firmly, and tack in place. Glue a piece of wet kraft paper to back of frame, allow it to dry and shrink, then trim to the edge of frame.

Always keep pressed flower portraits in indirect light as fading may occur if they are exposed to bright light.

A very striking picture can be designed using pressed white flowers and silver gray foliages on a black velvet background. For this I would suggest a small dull black frame.

The Not-So-Lowly Marigold

On the left, a white lotus bowl is arranged with yellow butterfly snapdragons, marigolds and baby's breath to create a lasting summer arrangement. On the right, marigolds, daisies and Queen Anne's lace are the right textured flowers to combine in an openwork Madeira basket.

The marigold is probably one of the most easily cultivated and most satisfactory annual flowers growing on our continent today. Too, it is very satisfactory when dried causing few, if any, of the problems found in drying many other flowers. It remains crisp and firm, retaining its beautiful colorations without the usual fading and is very easy to prepare prior to and after the drying process. High humidity does not "wilt" the properly prepared blooms and they hold up quite well if touched with inquisitive fingers. Hence my reason for devoting one section to this particular flower.

Marigolds were found growing in ancient Mexico by Cortez who took the seeds back to Spain. The devout Spanish grew them to place at the altar of the Virgin Mary; hence, they were called Mary's Gold and later named marigold. The plantsmen in Europe and America have, over the years, developed beautiful varieties of this jewel of the garden. In America, Burpee Seed Company has focused a great deal of attention on this flower, and they offer a wide selection in their seed catalog.

The marigold has been praised in prose and poetry by Shakespeare, by the Devonshire poet John Gay in 1685, by John Keats in 1821, by Thomas Hyll, author of the earliest book on gardening printed in the English language, plus countless other writers and poets.

Marigolds have played an important role in medicine. The dried flowers, finely powdered then mixed with honey, were considered a specific for depressed spirits and melancholy.

A tea steeped from the fresh or dried petals quieted the palpitation of the heart. Steeping the petals in vinegar, then rubbing the liquid on the gums relieved toothache. For a feverish cold, the fresh flowers were used for a hot tea to promote perspiration and to break up the cold. Poultices were made of flowers and leaves, boiled together, mashed and applied to burns, bruises and wounds to prevent gangrene and to promote healing.

The marigold flowers have long been known to contain an ingredient in their juice which stopped the flow of blood from a wound. During World War I many of the great estate gardens of England were turned over entirely to the raising of marigold. The flowers were sent to the first aid stations in France to be used as dressing for the wounds of the soldiers.

In English country districts, a syrup is made from honey and marigold petals and used to treat ulcers of the mouth.

Even today some doctors prescribe marigold ointment as a mild soothing salve for skin irritations. Pharmaceutical companies manufacture a fluid extracted from the marigold which is used to treat indigestion.

Our late Senator Dirksen of Illinois fought vigorously to designate the marigold as our national flower. At first I scoffed at his thinking, but then began to realize that here is a flower that will grow and bloom profusely in all our fifty states yet has never been selected as an official flower from any state. Perhaps that is the reason it holds its cheerful and brilliant head so high—just hoping that someday it will be crowned our national flower. If you agree, write to your senator or congressman. Perhaps the lowly marigold will not always be considered so lowly!

And now we turn to the culinary qualities of the marigold. This flower is often known as pot marigold because of its many uses in cookery. The brilliant yellow petals have been used to color butter, cheese, soups, breads and cakes. An old-time recipe for Marigold Pudding calls for the finely chopped petals mixed with bread crumbs, cream, egg and honey. Recipes of today include Marigold Rice, Marigold Chowder, Marigolden Cauliflower, Eggs Marigold,

Marigold Sweet Buns, Marigolden Custard, Marigold Cake and Marigold Dip. Recipes for the last two items are shared here with you.

MARIGOLD CAKE

    ½ c. butter
    1½ c. sugar
     6 egg yolks
     3 c. cake flour
     4 t. baking powder
    ½ t. salt
     1 c. milk
     2 T. finely crumbled dried marigold petals
     1 t. vanilla extract
     1 t. lemon extract

Cream butter and sugar until soft and fluffy. Beat egg yolks and add to butter-sugar mixture, beating well. Mix and sift together flour, baking powder and salt. Add alternately with milk. Add marigold petals, vanilla and lemon extracts and mix well. Pour into a greased and floured 9″ x 13″ pan and bake at 375° for 25 to 30 minutes.

The old recipe calls for no frosting on the cake, but a little confectioner's sugar may be sifted over the top.

MARIGOLD DIP

     1 8-oz. pkg. cream cheese
     1 c. sour cream
     1 t. minced parsley
     1 t. grated onion
     1 T. fresh marigold petals, chopped finely
       Dash of garlic salt
       Few drops Worcestershire sauce
       (optional)

Combine all ingredients, mixing well. Refrigerate at least one hour before serving to blend flavors.

One of my mother's dearest friends was Marian Kimble who gave a program on marigolds for the Women's Association of our church. I must thank her for allowing me to use her papers for much of the information and recipes in this section, and I am sure it is of much interest to my readers.

Roadside and Native Materials

Nature provides a year-round wealth of fascinating materials along roadsides, hedgerows, in meadows and wooded areas and along the banks of lakes and streams—all waiting to be gathered and arranged.

From late summer through winter and early spring these gems of nature are usually found in their own dried state and need no further processing, except to trim away the undesirable foliage and cull out any damaged parts. These are good months to look for seed heads, pods, contorted vines and branches, cones and nuts, bark formations and clusters of dried fruits and berries. From late spring through summer and autumn, great varieties of grasses and seed heads in all stages of growth and colorations are produced. Collecting these materials helps develop an awareness of the vast reservoir of nature's materials that are within our very reach.

Many refer to these roadside materials as weeds. To the ardent collector and arranger they are known as "botanicals"—a much more elegant and dignified word, especially when they are artistically and beautifully arranged for everyone to enjoy.

Most of the "roadsideana" materials can be processed by the air-dry method as outlined in section one. Just a word of caution—when gathering it is best to wear gloves and long-sleeved garments, leaving little, if any, of the skin exposed to poisonous plant materials or anything that might cause minor irritations. After gathering and processing, be sure to wash the hands, arms and any exposed areas in a heavy sudsy solution. Whenever available, I use the old-fashioned Fels Naphtha soap or homemade soap with a lye base. One of the Ideals publications, *Crafts for Everyone* has an excellent recipe for a homemade lye-base soap. There are several lotions available that help relieve any skin irritation that might be caused by contact with these roadside botanicals.

Most of the roadside materials used in the arrangements in this section were gathered in and around the Dixon, Illinois, countryside. Friends are always stopping by with materials they have gathered on trips, knowing that I can always use them in my arrangements or programs.

Be cautious when picking wild flowers or other native plant materials that might be protected by state law. Many states have a conservation list and laws regarding picking and transporting of native plants. It is not possible here to include one national conservation list or even one policy that would apply to all states. It might be best to write to your state conservation department before gathering any questionable or unfamiliar plant materials. When picking native plant materials, always allow some plants to remain in the ground so they may produce seed for the next season's crop. The conservation of our native plants is very important. Only you can help!

The wheel hub, used as a base for the arrangement of roadside material, was originally on a wagon train that came to Dixon in the 1850s.

On the left, bright marigolds combine with preserved
Scotch broom and privet arranged in a reproduction of an
early Grecian urn. On the right, marigolds and baby's
breath are combined with preserved goldenrod in a simple
clay pot and saucer compote.

Gourds: Growing and Curing

In my high school days in Princeton, Illinois, one of our English assignments was to write an essay. I chose "How to Grow and Cure Gourds," never realizing that nearly fifty years later I would include this same subject in a book. Growing gourds was one of my Grandfather Cook's hobbies; and I was quite sure his knowledge would be a great help to me—and it was. I received an "A" grade. So, I'll pass along his tips on growing and curing, plus some of my methods used in creating designs with gourds.

It might interest my readers to know that back in the thirties our group of young people would go out to Joe and Olive Crawford's farm nearly every night for a swim in their pool. After swimming, we would gather around a table and paint gourds, cones and pods. There were some mighty gaudy colors and effects! We made these into patio or fiesta strings and hung them along the front of one of Crawford's barns which housed their antique shop. As crude and colorful as they were, people bought them. One evening Joe and Olive suggested that I make the strings and sell them in a Christmas shop that I was planning to open in December 1938. This was the forerunner of my flower shop which I opened in January 1939. Olive Crawford, her two daughters and I often recall those happy, happy days.

Growing

Gourds must be planted early. I suggest starting the seeds of the *Lagenaria* variety in pots in a sunny windowsill garden, moving them to their permanent location after all danger of frost is over. The young plants are very tender and susceptible to the slightest

The fiesta string shows gourds, cones and milkweed pods brightly painted as we did in the thirties, wiring each of the items to an old hawser or baling twine. Preserved oak foliage is wired in clusters and used as a filler between the pods.

frost. Here in Dixon, Illinois, I plant the seeds in pots about the 10th of April, allowing a week or ten days for germination, then replant them in the garden after the 20th of May. By the way, there are two families of gourds, namely the *Lagenarias* that are large hard-shelled types generally used for dippers, birdhouses, bowls, etc. and the *Cucurbita* that are usually smaller and warty and are used in arrangements, wreaths, and swags. The George W. Park Seed Company in Greenwood, South Carolina 29647, has a wide variety of gourd seeds.

Gourds like a rich, heavy soil. My grandfather would spade well-rooted stable manure deep into the soil before transplanting them. His dipper and birdhouse gourds were a perennial winner at the county fair; and his ribbons were proudly displayed just below the plate rail on one of the kitchen walls. During a dry summer he would water and feed his plants with "manure-water." This was made by placing a burlap bag of manure in a tub of rainwater, allowing it to ripen for several days. Later he would dilute it with an equal amount of water from the cistern. If you want to stay on good terms with close neighbors, I suggest you substitute one of the modern-day commerical fertilizers, especially the time-release type for summer feeding.

Dipper and birdhouse gourds should be grown on a fence or support to allow the neck to stretch as the gourd develops weight. When grown on the ground, the gourd neck has a tendency to grow in a curve. Most of the other ornamental gourds can be grown on the ground and will mature into interesting shapes.

Curing

Allow the gourds to hang on the vines through two or three good frosts. Cut the stem off close to the vine, leaving about three or four inches on the gourd. Let them dry in a cool place, either hanging or placing on a screen or rack, turning them occasionally. It takes several months for them to dry and for the seeds to rattle. They develop a mold-type coating which is easily removed by lightly scouring with an abrasive cleanser or scouring pad. Oftentimes the yellow green and orange beige colorations remain and are interesting to use in some designs. After they are cured and cleaned, they can be colored with nearly any dye, stain or paint.

To make dippers, birdhouses or bowls, select a suitable gourd and choose a place for the opening, circling the area with a pencil line. With a very sharp knife, start a hole in the center; then slowly and cautiously cut through the shell of the gourd, trimming outwardly to the penciled line. Remove the pulp and seeds and smooth the edges with a fine file, sandpaper or steel wool. To hang the curved gourd, drill two holes near the top of the gourd and run a wire, cord or baling twine through the holes to form a hanger.

Alternate freezing and thawing will hasten the curing and drying process for the large gourds. These can be hung outside or placed in the freezer to simulate nature's process. Even if they become soft and mushy after thawing, they will eventually dry and develop a hard shell.

Gourds are fascinating. Grow some in your garden and watch them mature into interesting shapes. Then have fun curing them for decorations!

Photo right: The wreath at the top right of the picture is made of gourds, preserved foliages, cones and pods on a straw wreath frame. The gourds were colored with a fruitwood stain, but the other materials are used in their natural color. Below and to the right of the wreath is a wooden tray filled with dried gourds, bittersweet and carrion berries combined with preserved Mountain Ash berries and foliage.

The arrangement in the lower right-hand corner of the picture is in a dipper gourd. This gourd was grown on a fence and has a straight handle. It serves as a suitable container for a table arrangement of berries, pods and grasses. To the left of the gourd and lying on the floor is an example of a gourd grown on the ground. Growth resulted in curving the gourd, making it a fine example of a dipper gourd.

All About Corn

Corn is truly beautiful—first the tiny sprouts of green begin to emerge and form long straight rows in field after field. Then come the chartreuse green tassels with the ears and corn silk forming on the stalk. And in the autumn, the grand finale of beautiful fields of bleached beige tones with the golden ears clinging tenaciously to the stalk, seemingly waiting for the pickers to arrive. Finally the long trip to the processors and the marketplaces to help feed a very hungry world. Yes, corn is beautiful!

Corn played an important part in the founding of our great country. Massasoit, the Wampanoag Indian Chief, brought grains of corn to the starving Plymouth Colony in Massachusetts in the spring of 1621 and instructed the colonists in the planting of the corn. Later that year the colonists gathered with the friendly Indians for a thanksgiving feast, a custom that more or less became an annual event throughout the New England area. A national day for offering thanks was first proclaimed in 1784. In 1863 Abraham Lincoln set a date for a national harvest festival and in 1864 he proclaimed the last Thursday of November as a day of nationwide Thanksgiving. So, it all began with a few grains of corn and a grateful group of Indians and colonists.

The ears of field corn, especially the calico or Indian corn, offer a variety of decorative uses. The New Englanders would hang a swag of corn at their gates or their doorways to denote the harvest season. Today we go to great efforts to design appealing decorations for the doorway as a greeting for our guests or passersby. An arrangement of two or three ears of corn combined with some preserved oak foliage and sprays of bittersweet or other berries or pods adds a cheery greeting to the entranceway. An antique corn drier with corn and other decoratives could be used on a wall or a large door. The ears of corn are impaled on the points of the drier and a decorative cluster secured to the top and center. If you must have ribbon, use burlap, sisal or braided baling twine. Never use satin ribbon with corn!

In this section I will show and discuss the many decorative uses of this important agricultural product—the stalk, husk, ears, cob, tassel and even the corn silk.

Tassels

A farmer friend will be happy to let you gather some of the corn tassels. Select them in various stages of color, from the fresh light green through the dry beige tones. Tie in small bunches and hang from the rafters to dry. If desired, these tassels can be tinted by using a floral spray paint. I prefer to use the muted autumn tones for the tassels, as shown in the photograph on page 52. I usually cut the tassel with a short stem and make an extended stem by adding an 18 gauge wire, tipped with Quik glue and inserted in the center of the stem end. After the glue has dried I bind the wire stem with floratape.

Corncobs

Corncobs can be used to make people or animal figurines. The two cob figurines shown on page 52 were brought by friends to my hospital room and evoked much laughter, conversation and cheer. The card reads: "So you think you have troubles? I've been picked, shucked and shelled. But baby, look at me now!" Placed next to me on my bedside table they brought many smiles and I'm certain hastened my recovery. All it takes is a good imagination and adept fingers to create this type of design.

Cornstalks

Cornstalks make an excellent background screen for your designs, rivaling the oftentimes difficult-to-find bamboo. The stalks can be gathered in nearly any stage of growth. Those shown in the photograph were brought in from the field in April, just before the farmer began the spring field work. I stripped the stalk of all the dried foliage and scrubbed each stalk with a scouring pad in warm soapy water. Steel wool or stronger abrasives generally remove any stubborn stains. Rinse thoroughly and remove excess water with cloth or paper towels. Place on a flat surface and allow to dry. I often use a provincial oak wood stain with an overcoat of dull varnish on the stalks to be used as backgrounds or mats for Oriental-style arrangements.

Corn husks

Corn husks have been used for centuries for both cooking and doll making. The Mexicans use the husks in cooking their tamales. Indians made little primitive corn husk dolls for their children. Later the Appalachian folk made corn husk flowers. All these uses of the corn husk are very much alive today.

Proper gathering, preparing and storing the husks prior to their use is a very important step in the success you will have in creating these interesting and decorative corn husk flowers.

Ears of Indian corn and apples are impaled on a corn drier for a festive wall or door decoration.

Photo opposite, beginning at lower center and moving clockwise: The crockery container holds an arrangement of cornhusk roses and dried baby's breath. Cornhusk magnolia flowers and forsythia are arranged with preserved magnolia leaves in a low wooden salad bowl.

On the chest are two corncob figures and an old scale scoop which holds an arrangement of corn tassels, cornhusk daises and calico corn. On the wall, an antique corn dryer holds ears of calico corn with cluster of wheat and cornhusk roses as an accent.

On the chair are the elements of a wedding. My friends, Judy and Steve Thomas, were married along the shore of a lake on her sister's farm in southern Illinois. Her bouquet of cornhusk roses, baby's breath and other dried materials complemented her polyester cotton gauze and lace ankle-length wedding dress. A few cornhusk roses were attached to her wide-brimmed hat. On the chest of drawers you will note the cornhusk rose corsages worn by the mothers and the boutonnieres worn by the fathers. The attendants carried French flower baskets arranged with complementary dried materials. A long-to-be-remembered wedding!

Corn husks soaking in a solution of glycerine and warm water.

Preserving and Tinting Corn Husks

If you are using husks from the corn field, try to gather them before the corn is picked. A farmer friend might let you gather husks after he brings his harvested crop into the storage area. The husks should be dry before gathering. The cleanest husks are those closest to the ear of corn. When gathering the husks remove the husk at the stem end, as the end has heavier ridges to support the petals. This area of the husk is excellent for the flower centers. Dusty or soiled husks can be washed in a warm water solution containing liquid soap and bleach, then placed out in the sun to dry. When completely dried they can then be stored for future use.

I always add about 3 tablespoons of glycerine to each quart of warm water to soak the husks before using them. This helps keep them soft

and pliable while working with them. They are difficult to work with if too wet, and split or crack if too dry. After removing the husks from the solution I place them between sheets of paper towels to remove excess moisture and retain a soft, pliable texture.

You can tint the husks by placing them in a solution of warm water containing either household fabric dye or vegetable food coloring. The floral sprays are also a very handy method of coloring. It is better to use the floral spray after the flower is constructed and completely dry.

Follow the step-by-step procedures until you develop a method that is best suited for you. Soon you will be recreating many of your favorite flowers from corn husks. It's fun, it's challenging, it's creative! Enjoy it!

Corn Husk Daisy Instructions

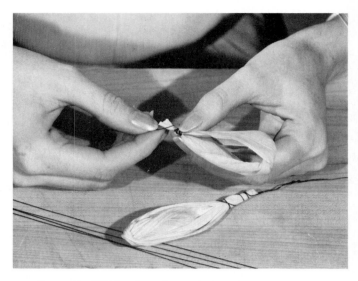

Step 1. Prepare husks by soaking them in warm water and glycerine. Add two or three tablespoons glycerine per quart of water. Allow husks to soak until they are soft and pliable.

Step 3. With thumb and forefinger of each hand grasp center of husk strip and make the two complete twists, folding one half over the top of lower half, tightly pinching the two ends and binding with a fine wire or heavy thread. The petals can now be shaped into desired form while the husks are soft and pliable. Some can be stretched and formed to make wide petals while others can be folded close together to make narrow petals.

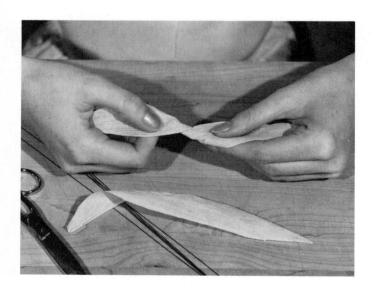

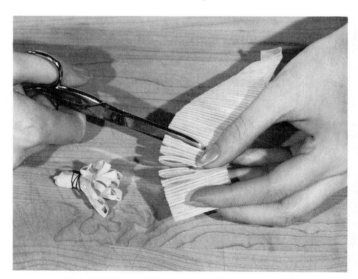

Step 2. Tear or cut husks into strips varying from 1 to 2 inches wide and 6 to 10 inches long. Cut or tear with the grain of the husk. Taper ends of wider strips to 1 inch.

Step 4. To make the center stamens cut 4 inch lengths of wide husks. Fold this piece cross grain with a very sharp fold. With a scissors cut very narrow fringe-like incisions about 1 inch deep across the length of the folded husk.

Step 5. Roll the fringed strip and bind with fine wire or thread. Add additional fringed strips if a larger center is desired.

Step 6. To form the stem insert a previously florataped and glue tipped 16 or 18 gauge wire into the middle of flower center and bind. At this point I generally floratape the base of the flower center and continue florataping the entire length of the wire stem. Determine the gauge of the wire stem by the support needed to hold the flower in position. The length of the wire stem should be determined by the length needed when the flower is placed in the arrangement. I usually use an 18 inch length and then cut it if a shorter stem is needed or floratape an extra wire of heavier gauge to the stem if a longer stem is desired.

Step 7. While the petals are still soft and pliable place a row of shorter petals around the center and bind to the flower stem with fine wire or thread. Repeat the same method with a second or third row of petals depending on the desired size of the flower. Increase the length of petals with each succeeding row.

Step 8. Cover the base of the final row of bound flower petals with several binds of masking tape. Cover the masking tape and binding wires with floratape. I generally use twig green or brown color floratape for all corn husk flowers.

Corn Husk Rose Instructions

Step 1. Soak husks in pan of warm water, adding two or three tablespoons glycerine per quart of water. Allow husks to remain in solution until they are soft and pliable.

Step 2. Form the center of the flower by cutting a piece of the husk, 2 inches square. With the ridged side of the husk down and the smooth side up, make a sharp half-inch fold across the grain of the husk and roll so that the turned-down edge will be on the inside and form the top edge of the rose center. Bind the base with a length of fine wire.

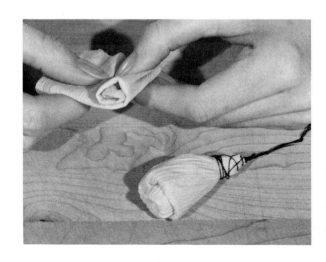

56

Step 3. Form the stem by inserting a florataped and glue tipped 16 or 18 gauge wire into the middle of the flower center and bind. Floratape the base of the flower center and continue taping the entire length of the wire stem. The gauge of the wire stem can be determined by the support needed to hold the flower in position. The length of the stem should be determined by the length needed when the flower is placed in the arrangement. I usually use an 18 inch length and then cut it if a shorter stem is needed.

Step 4. With a tracing paper, outline the three actual size patterns and cut a template out of heavy paper or light cardboard. Use this template as a pattern and cut 6 small, 5 medium and 4 large petals. Always cut with the ridges or grains running straight to the top of the pattern. Cut the patterns and work with the petals while the husks are soft and pliable. If the petals become brittle, replace in solution until they are again soft and pliable. Any excess solution can be blotted with a paper towel.

Step 6. Place one of the smaller petals around the flower center, gathering the pointed ends together, forming the petals into shape with your thumb. Add another petal, overlapping the previous one about one fourth. Continue this same procedure until all six petals are in place. Bind in place with a fine wire and wrap excess wire down on the florataped stem. Wrap the base of these first petals and stem with floratape.

Step 5. To curl the petals, roll the curved parts around a lead pencil or draw the dull side of a silver knife tightly across the underside of the petals. The heavy ribbed side must be downside.

Step 7. Continue the same procedure with the 5 medium-size petals, bind and floratape. The 4 large petals are then placed, formed, bound and florataped.

Step 1. Soak husks in warm water and glycerine, using two or three tablespoons glycerine per quart of water, until they are soft and pliable. Using tracing paper, outline the four actual-size patterns and cut a template out of heavy paper or light cardboard. Using this template as a pattern, cut 3 small inner petals, 1 flower center, 2 medium and 1 large petal from corn husks.

Step 2. Form flower center by pleating, pinching and rolling one of the ends along the grain of the husk. Bind with fine wire.

Step 3. Very carefully pull the untied ends down over the outside and even with the bottom of the rolled husk, forming a center for the flower. Bind with fine wire and floratape. Add a flower stem, inserting a florataped and glue tipped 16 or 18 gauge wire into the middle of the center and bind to the end of the wire.

Instructions for Making Corn Husk Magnolia Flowers

Step 4. Place the three smaller inner petals around flower center, overlapping each petal about one-third around the flower center and stem. Pleat each petal at the base and cup inwardly. Bind and floratape. I find it much easier to separately bind and tape each petal. Repeat with the two medium petals and, finally, the single large petal. These petals must be extra soft and pliable in order to pleat and form a natural appearing cup-shaped magnolia flower.

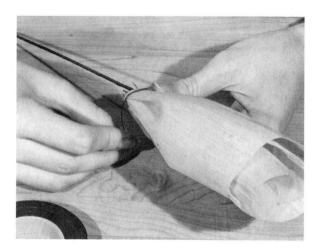

Step 5. Brown preserved natural magnolia leaves can then be bound and florataped to the stem. These leaves are generally available at florists, garden centers or craft shops. Or you can preserve your own.

The corn husk magnolia flowers are not as simple to make as either the daisy or rose. Neither is it as easy to describe the procedure. Read and study the directions and accompanying photographs before starting the project. For those with absolutely no creative talents I suggest you order the magnolia flowers from The Log House, Berea College Student Craft Industries, Berea, Kentucky 40404, but at least try! Who knows, it might bring out your hidden talent.

Small inner petal (cut 3)

Flower center (cut 1)

Medium petal (cut 2)

Large petal (cut 1)

The door wreath, is designed on an 18-inch reinforced straw wreath frame and consists of dried goldenrod, wild yarrow, assorted grasses, milkweed pods, hedge apples and hedge apple flowers, bittersweet (the chartreuse plums at top center are sumac picked early). Preserved pear and beech foliage are used for accent.

The door basket is an old garden caddy set in a maple sugarin'-off pail and is filled with dried foxtail grass, milkweed pods, teasel and contrived hedge apple flowers combined with preserved goldenrod.

Maclura pomifera is the Latin name for the tree producing these large, attractive fruits in the fall. The common names of hedge apple or Osage orange relates to the fact that years ago they were planted as hedges to denote property lines and the skin of the fruit has the appearance of an orange.

They are fast growing, very thorny trees and the early settlers planted them for hedges as they made excellent barriers and the cattle would not penetrate them.

The very attractive chartreuse green fruit is scarcely noticeable until late in the fall after the leaves have dropped. I would certainly not recommend that this tree be planted near a lawn or public areas as its littering habit is very objectionable and being struck by a fallen fruit could prove to be a very painful experience.

As you drive along the countryside in the autumn you can generally spot groups of these fruit-laden trees. Any property owner is usually happy to give you permission to gather the fallen fruit. Be sure and wear a hard hat if you try to shake the tree or try to knock them off with a long pole. Their thorns will stop anyone from climbing the branches.

There is an old wive's tale that a few of these fruit placed in the cellar in the fall will keep the field mice away. The only use I have found for the fruit is in making attractive flowers or drying them and combining with other dried materials in creating interesting arrangements and wreaths.

If you are fortunate to find some uprooted Osage orange trees, pay particular attention to the very interesting orange-colored roots. You might possibly find some gnarled, twisted roots that can be severed, dried and used in some of your designs.

Here's an interesting anecdote that might bring a chuckle. During one of the fall programs I was presenting before a very large regional garden club meeting, I was using the Osage oranges in an autumn arrangement combined with other harvest materials. Unthinkingly I referred to them as "road apples" instead of "hedge apples." I noticed there were quite a few chuckles from the audience. Completely

Hedge Apple Flowers

unaware of my first error I repeated it several times until a very kind lady in the second or third row, still smiling and with a loud and clear whisper said "Mr. Cook, I hope you realize there is a difference between a hedge apple and a road apple." The audience laughed and it took me several minutes to regain my composure. Only those who recall the horse and buggy days will appreciate this story! And, be assured, I've been very careful not to repeat this blunder.

In this section I will discuss and explain the procedure to follow in making these flowers and show how they can be used as accents in several designs.

Drying

Besides slicing and baking to create contrived flowers, the whole hedge apple can be dried to use in wreaths and arrangements. This is a long, slow process but well worth all the time involved. I have used two methods, air drying and drying in silica gel.

To air dry, place the fruit on a mesh rack in a warm area. Turn the fruit every week or ten days until they are completely dry. Any mold that appears will eventually dry and can be scoured off with a household abrasive. By the time they have dried, their color will be a rich tone of brown.

One late autumn day I buried several hedge apples in silica gel in an airtight container and forgot about them until spring, nearly six months later. They were thoroughly dry and had not required the weekly turning ritual; and they, too, had a rich dark brown color. The silica gel had absorbed all the moisture and the usual blue indicator crystals had all turned white. The spent silica gel was restored to use by placing in a warm oven until the indicator crystals returned to their normal blue color.

Directions for Hedge Apple Flowers

Step 1. In addition to a supply of hedge apples assemble the few necessary materials required to make the completed flowers, namely: a very sharp serrated blade knife or electric knife, scissors, household foil, foil muffin cups and small pie pans, twig green or brown ½ inch floral tape, Quik glue, #24 gauge spool wire, cookie sheet and #16, #18, #20 gauge florists cut wire and milliners wire.

Step 2. Place foil on a cutting board and cut the hedge apples in slices ranging from ⅛ inch to ¼ inch thick. Suggest you wear an apron and have paper towels handy as this can be quite messy and sticky.

Step 3. With a scissors score the edges. This will create a petal-like appearance after they are baked.

Step 4. Place some of the slices flat on a foil-covered cookie sheet and fold others into the muffin cups. Place in 250° oven and bake until they have reached the desired color. I prefer several stages of coloration, ranging from chartreuse green to dark brown.

Step 5. Remove from oven when they are baked to suit you, transfer to another foil covered sheet and allow to cool and dry.

Step 6. Attaching a wire to form a stem can be accomplished in several ways. Sometimes I form an L-shaped hook on the end of a length of #16 or #18 gauge milliners wire. Tip this end with fast drying glue and hold firmly against the center of the reverse side of the flower until the glue has set and hardened. There are many fast setting craft glues available. Or I use my electric glue gun—dropping a bit of glue on the flower and pressing the stem into the hot glue for a few moments until it is set.

Step 7. A small teasel pod, a small cluster of rust tinted tansy, yellow yarrow or other dried material that resembles a stamen can be wired and inserted in the center. If you are going to add the flower center it would be best to make a hole in the center of the baked hedge apple with an ice pick or other pointed object as soon as it is removed from the oven and is still soft. If it is very dry and brittle I find it easier to drill a hole with a small hand or electric drill, as a punch or ice pick often cracks the flower. Insert the stem end of the wired flower center through the hole, and place a few drops of Quik glue around the hole before drawing the center tightly against the flower. Lay flowers with face side down to dry. When dry and firm add whatever gauge wire is necessary to support the flower and cover the stem with bindings of brown or twig green floral tape.

In Conclusion . . .

As I close this, my second book, I hope you have gained a greater awareness of the vast reservoir of native materials that is available for us to use. Even after years of collecting, drying and preserving, I continue to find many materials that I have overlooked. I've truly enjoyed writing this book, designing the arrangements and selecting the backgrounds. Now I hope some of this enthusiasm will inspire you to enjoy this fascinating hobby. Have a happy time!

Here is one example of combining dried flowers from the marketplace with home-preserved ones. Orange cardones, lagurus and clusters of hill flowers are arranged with preserved eucalyptus and baby's breath.

About the Author

After a busy and rewarding career in the gardening field as a guest lecturer for design schools in many states, as a lecturer in major universities and at annual garden club conventions, and after the publication of his first book on his favorite subject, Decorating for the Holidays, Harold C. Cook is now devoting all his time, energy and talents to the writing of books and articles on the many phases of this fascinating subject.

In this, his second book, Creating Designs with Dried Flowers, Harold Cook, a native of Illinois, continues to interest his many readers and friends in the preserving, drying and arranging of flowers, leaves, and seed heads, and tells us how these materials may be used for our own enjoyment to decorate our homes.

How often is information by an experienced designer made available to the public? In this book you will be able to make use of this valuable information, but perhaps more importantly, you will begin to absorb Harold Cook's enthusiasm for nature's handiwork.

As this publication goes to press, we have learned of the untimely death of Harold C. Cook. We hope that to Mr. Cook's many friends and students, this book will serve as a reminder of the author's continued dedication to beauty through nature.